Triple No. 5

Tree Riesener
Nina Corwin
Jason Gordon

The Ravenna Triple Series
*Chapbooks as they were meant to be read—
in good company.*

Copyright © Ravenna Press, 2017
All rights reserved, reverting on publication to the individual authors

ISBN: 978-0-9995921-0-6

Published by Ravenna Press
USA
ravennapress.com

First Edition

Angel Fever
  by Tree Riesener   *page* 1

Outpatient Suite
  by Nina Corwin   *page* 47

Attack of the Nihilist
  by Jason Gordon   *page* 71

Acknowledgments & Biographies

Tree Riesener

Angel Fever

angel fever

according to
the celestial hierarchies by dionysius
and s*umma theologica* by aquinas
they both agree
nine celestial orders
orbit the throne of glory
seraphim cherubim thrones
dominations virtues powers
principalities archangels angels
like an aquarium
of mixed tropical fish
swimming back and forth
at different levels
swishing filmy fins and tails
suddenly dashing up
in a glory of translucent filament
then sinking like corpses
down to the bottom-feeding catfish
you must please swim gracefully
you angels in heaven
lovely fish
although you can breathe
out of water
know that the nine circles
of status and envy
will be your downfall

highest triad

first choir seraphim

well
you speak only
to god
sing creation
one each for
east west north south
not so many of you
six wings four heads
serpents of lightning
addicted
to angelic extreme makeovers
regularly
shedding your wings
like snakeskins
appearing
in ever more brilliant pinions
discarded husks
like last year's fashions
over aeons
drift slowly to earth
curious faded objects
that occasionally in the sun
glint of colors

not before seen on earth
collected in the desert
by elderly couples
draped with turquoise
following the sun in motor homes

how long
will you be satisfied
even with heavenly bodies
where will it end

second choir cherubim

marlon brando enforcers
sons and daughters
lumped together
in so many songs
cherubim and seraphim
that's like we the people
we're all equal
but some of us
are more equal than others
doomed forever
to carry out the tough stuff
smash and destroy
decadent cities
wrench open
heavenly taps

see fire
rained on occasion
tear families apart
for slavery in babylon
I am so happy
for your image change
if you're sure
that's what you want

but how did you
of the four faces
four wings
flaming swords in eden
become small chubby beings
pastel backgrounds for e-mail

third choir thrones

you
who burn with lightning
chrysolitic vision
blessed flying unicycles
flaming wheels
patron saints
of hell's angels
and the elderly on tricycles
in gated communities
both chariots and charioteers

you exemplify
who are the dancers
who are the dance
in your monster-wheeled vehicles
waaaay above the traffic
in the third and fourth heavens
there where sky meets earth
where the marvelous
face-lifting moisturizer
is on the shelf without prescription
ezekiel the celebrity spokesperson

do you mourn your lost dignity
proud name become supporters only

middle triad

fourth choir dominations

administrators
of the other angels
once channels of mercy
bestowers of blessings
now you are
the patrons of dungeons
chains and spanking
your very name

a warning light
to peaceful lives
occasions for marital counseling
suppliers of military academies
for future dictators
of third-world countries
eaters of energy
vast bulky angels
squeezed into your modern garb
maybe yearning for
but not allowed
laura ashley
glass menageries

in your tight-laced corsets
whips instead of swords
six-inch heels
are you wistfully envious
of the great peacock-eyed pinions
or the re-born cherubim

fifth choir virtues

present
at the ascension
to escort
christ to heaven
after satan

had his comeuppance
fond of miracles
not always subtle
but good-hearted
there for people
facing dismissal
having babies
dying
one of you judas' guardian angel
eve's midwives
at the birth of cain
chose not to smother
spanked cain to life
knowing
life's life where you find it
who knows
if a decision will be made
passive voice
an alternate map
bound
into the triptych
ours not to question why
into the jaws of death
rode the six hundred

did you have a choice
or were you damned
in spite of never asking to be born

sixth choir powers

demon pimps
bottom-out standards
lovers for any comers
twelve-step programs
would improve your souls
but when you're good
you're very very good
the border patrol
between heaven and hell
if we follow directions
from an old yard sale paperback
get lost
in the astral plane
you're the ones
we want on our side
angelic st. bernards
out searching
for the tentatively damned
bread and wine
strapped around your necks
as we waver
between good and evil
condemned to be principals
micro-managers
shift supervisors at macdonald's
listeners-in on telemarketers

for training purposes only sure
but
when
you find us in the snowdrift
you know how
to stuff us with bread
like we're foie-gras geese
pour wine down our throats
until we know we're saved

you children
in the middle
reconciliators
peacemakers
conflicted
have you done your enneagram
your myers-briggs
is career change in the offing

<u>lowest triad</u>

seventh choir principalities

closest to us
like chimps
but you're on top
sharing all

but one chromosome with us
again like the chimps
we walk the line
between
animal
human
monsters
butchers
saints
and rage
which are we most like
them or you
do we waver back and forth
protectors of religion
not very imaginative
go by the book
interested in cooking
on the flames of hell
barbecue masters with leather aprons
your dominion the moon
and as far as the big apple

how do you like
being the newly-authorized
patron saint of dolly the cloned
the monster of the labyrinth

eighth choir archangels

of ozzy emerald wings
each of your saffron hairs
with a million faces
and mouths
and tongues
imploring
the pardon of god
in a million dialects
charon's the psychopomp
but you're bus conductors
airline couriers
gabrielle the lone archangel girl
among the guys
token yes
but maybe everybody's crossdressing
or at least unisex
you angels of truth
but notably
not without a sense of humor
needed
for your hundred forty pairs of wings
announcers of childbirth
baby shower saints
teachers of souls *in utero*
those lessons
the trailing clouds of glory
alas soon lost

archangels
do you struggle
not to call the angels
rednecks
trailer trash

ninth choir angels only angels

three hundred and one million
six hundred and fifty five thousand
seven hundred and twenty-two of you
created anew every morning
when god breathes
does god breathe
that many times
each morning
and when does morning end
at everybody's beck and call
bullied and harassed
bitches
of the heavenly cell block
eleven thousand for every child
and one for every blade of grass
lowest of the lowest three
homely our visitors
you run errands
get into trouble

guardians of cities towns and people
why not cheat for your charges
you've been known to
will
kill
for us
it's a matter of record
even among the angel proles
there are classes the two-eyed serpent angels
straw bosses
middle management
cyclopean angels
each supervising 496,000 colleagues
yes do your math
finally the ones we see
here and there healing paper cuts
why not tempt damned adam and eve
on a boring thursday afternoon
raid the fridge
give them that leftover piece of
triple chocolate mousse with mocha cream

did you know
the boss was saving
that one for a snack
or was it just an apple

and as you live
your aeons through

maybe not an aquarium
bound in brightness
maybe the lake
that's round the earth
you think
you'll swim
in the rain
the gentle mist
torrential flood flung down
or paddle in the blue water
of abandoned quarries
sometimes milky soft water
cooling even to angelic skin
that lives too close
but then you hit
the deep black cold
of spots where dragons in the water
wait
pull out in time
and gradually let
your air-dried feathers
float again
decide to swim
through soil
through rocks
through molten lava
people
power lines
television

rock and roll
like worms
passing every grain of earth
through their humble bodies
until such labor
makes our globe all fertile fine
so you
your expiatory tasks
will burnish bright again
until you're new-born
angels fish or worms

secret angel

my secret angel strips so well
he makes adultery a real pleasure
I can't say it's a matter of concentration on his part
because the least little thing distracts him
like those tiny bumps on my nipples
the way my elbow hinges work
a new color of nail polish
dust on the carved headboard
or the cat jumping on the bed
then it's ooh and aah and did you see that
as he spreads his wings
and zips around the room
in a kind of ecstacy
wings pulsing a transparent aura
like an old wurlitzer juke box
the one with bubble lights and rotating color
   columns
that radiance falls across my naked body
like the flashing neon bar sign
outside a hot-sheet hotel
all I have to do is
take a deep breath
sip some champagne
stretch out on the bed so the sheets whisper a little
shoot a shower of perfume in the air

so it falls on my body like fragrant rain
and he's right there with me again
never loses his interest
comes back more pumped up than ever
he's so in love with everything
that everything becomes a part
of what happens in that room
remember the amazing technicolor dreamcoat
well forget that and think about
a strawberries-with-heavy-cream-
butterscotch-candy-hot-mint-tea-
supple-fragrant-silk-rough-pine-needle-bed-
under-a-sliver-of-translucent-canned-pear-
moon-sobbing-in-the-movies-on-Saturday-
afternoon-choosing-the-softest-fabric-to-line-
your-mother's-coffin-piles-of-good-books-
stacked-up-for-winter-
mouthful-of-snowflakes orgasm and you'll have
just the tiniest idea of what it's like
adultery with an angel

evening prayer

standing outside the windows
you might have thought the place on fire

champagne-fizzy summoned light
lapped in the door
gold shaded to amber
lighter streams like summer hair
or scotch swirling around ice cubes

trickle soon gave way
to tide swooshing over the carpet
sucking back leaving trails of light foam
one surge hit the opposite wall
curled up and over
like the wave in that japanese print
spraying faces drenching clothes
knocking us onto our knees

the walls began to glow
steady sunset inch by inch
gilded the absorbent air
the ceiling opened up
like the skylight of a car
barreling down the malibu parkway
light came crashing down

so we scrabbled in bags
took out tissues
scrubbed our faces clean of protection

the lightning rod
stood steady in our midst
light-soaked gorgeous robes clinging
like a traffic cop like a conductor
laughing at all the swirling all the light
all the slooshy blessing

cupping the harmony
catching golden zingers
in an embroidered baseball mitt
dribbling sun like a basketball star
splashing big handfuls of healing on our
　heads
niagara falls for our wounds
lavish and unexpected

on that ordinary thursday evening
in the animal-decorated children's chapel
it was a different kind of flood

the magi asleep in st. lazare cathedral
on a capital in the nave
an angel awaking them

"Aske for those Kings whom thou saw'st yesterday,
  And thou shalt hear, All here in one bed lay."
        John Donne, *The Sunne Rising*

under the star
sleeping all three side by side
covered up to their necks
hats on or maybe some sort of nightcaps
one right arm drifted outside the circular cover

is the angel is tucking them in snugly
like a mother on a cold winter night
making sure they'll stay warm

actually no
the dream of peril
has failed to awaken them
and so they need the gentle touch
of one angelic finger

shhhh rise quickly dress eat
get on the road again
under the star
traveling on camels it took them a long time

to find the miracle
they slept out many nights along the way

imagine you have a sign
that something wonderful is out there
might even save the world
problem is you have no idea what to look for
or how long it will take
all you know is you'll be on the road
for a good long time
you need trustworthy company
for any sort of road trip
you thank god you've got good buddies

still you have to raise capital
expeditions of this sort are costly

never knowing what climate
what sort of terrain you'll be coping with
you've got to be prepared
that means funding
which involves tv rights and logos
vehicles provisioning
water gear climbing gear desert gear
warm clothes cool clothes
sunblock
bottled water and a purifier

some of that powdered water
from the mountain store
might not be a bad idea
although it costs an arm and a leg
shoes
you can't put too much thought
or money into shoes
shoes are central

nobody likes to mention it
but quietly slipped on board
some protection
rifles sidearms knives
how about a cyanide pill for last extremities
would that be showing lack of faith
no need for a video camera
not with the cnn rep along
multi-talented kid who can handle a humvee
cook and knows martial arts
in that non-showy way you can trust

the day comes
you're all wearing your good luck socks
one red one green
and you've taken a vow
to wear the same combination
(although not the same socks)
throughout the trip
you've each got one of those explorer's vests

with eleven million pockets
for cameras and compasses and candy

melchior
the thoughtful one
is sitting crosslegged
in his prayer posture

caspar
the best dreamer the visionary
the one who first had the dream
and urged the others to dream it
is packing his adventures stories
how he knows what mistakes scott made
shackleton livingstone

balthazar
the conscientious one with the clipboard
the star charts
the topographic maps
is reading the manual
for the computer positioning gadget

finally you crack a bottle of bubbly
on the front humvee and splash it
into plastic glasses
that are put into a manila envelope and labeled
let the documentation begin

the first rule is frequent meetings
anybody can call a meeting

whenever they think
they have something to consider
say you're driving through kansas
you start seeing signs about a cathedral
somebody's built
out of soda cans and marbles
eighth wonder of the world
furthermore it's midsummer night's eve
you remember how the sunlight
striking through the door at stonehenge
points the way to something
well you can propose that
you make a little detour and check it out
chances are it won't be anything
but once you've got there
interviewed the proprietor
marveled at the amount of soda they drank to
  make it
although friends saved up their cans too
you've got the backup
you check the star
is the star standing still
if it is you unpack and look around
until you find what you're supposed to find

maybe a little towheaded kid
running around the cathedral barefoot
with a squirt gun
is the one who's going to save the world
you'll be the first ones to document that
well you'd kick yourself if you passed that up
and some other expedition
some other network got there first
so you walk with the kid
over to momma's refreshment stand

ask if you can buy him a fudgesicle
talk to the kid sprawled there on the grass
ask about his momma and daddy
do unusual things ever happen to him
when he's playing
like modeling birds out of clay
and then they take off flying
or accidentally killing a playmate
who's been bullying him
by just thinking about it

disappointing
then that night you look up
see the star farther along than the night before
realize it had just been a temporary glitch
or maybe tired eyes
you alert everybody
and the next morning

after coffee and doughnuts
at the oasis there in kansas
you're on your way again

even though you've got the humvees
it's harder to follow a star
than you thought
you discover you can look to the north
see it
then turn around
and look to the south
still see it
the fancy gear gives you a bunch of numbers
you gravely consider
but in the end you agree just to go
as the spirit moves you
as long as the star seems farther along
so you spend a number of months on the road

there are many cathedrals
of soda cans and marbles
along the way
many cute little towheaded kids
for thorough researchers
it all takes a long time
fortunately with all the oases
to supply you with whoppers and slurpees

you haven't even tapped into
the freeze-dried meals
and have only had to use the water purifier
once in st. louis
when they were having
a municipal water emergency
night comes always a time
when the three of you feel discouraged
although you're still keeping up a bold front
for the expedition

you've got everybody rooms
in a cheap but spotlessly clean place
so they can shower and have some beers
the three of you are sitting
on the edge of the pool under the moon
when you hear a ruckus
at the registration desk
it's a mom and pop operation
and this guy from the pickup out front
has rung the bell

well you know what the proprietor is saying is true
because the expedition has taken over the whole motel
but the man is arguing
cracker from the sound of that provincial
　georgia accent
saying his wife is outside in the pickup
pregnant

he'll sleep in the truck bed
but could she just have the couch there in the lobby
you passed her in the truck as you went in
hardly more than a teenager
half asleep there in the truck
hell you're explorers
you're the three amigos and the buck stops here
so you offer to give up your room
the proprietor well he doesn't give a damn
not at that hour of the night
after she sees that nice room
with one king size bed and a cot
the three of you were going to make do with
you think the way she smiles at you
is all the riches of the world
and when a couple of hours later
you hear the proprietor and his wife
rushing around boiling water
you go to see what's up

the three of you go outside to smoke
under that huge steady star
you start to fill the bed of the pickup
with sleeping bags and freeze-dried food and
   extra socks
pool whatever cash you've got
even empty your pockets of change
to make up a little purse for them

that you leave on the front seat of the truck
for a surprise
then after you stand up as godfathers for the baby
you declare the expedition is over

you all agree it would be a good idea
to get on the road before dawn
just in case that cop that was dogging you
for having something not up to standard
on one of the humvees
and for being damnyankees
gets out an alert
a major fine and a night in jail
wouldn't be a good ending for the trip

might as well get started home
to argue with your sponsors
over whether or not you'd completed your mission
if you had to return any of the money
get started interviewing

you all end up with good jobs and nice families
keep in touch text message even call
on those days like christmas and easter
when for some reason
your mind goes back to your younger days
and after a while the conversation
always ends up on that night

the worried father
the strangely serene teenage mother
that nice little baby
you all agree you wish you knew how to get in touch
and hope life turned out okay for him

garden of eden

in later tales
they told in the freezing darkness
they wished the angel had been other

not like a bouncer at a trendy club
admitting and refusing
according to some secret rules only he knew

but waiting there happy to see them
these hard-to-handle children
who had fled their scolding
yet nevertheless were welcome to return

to soft white beds buttered toast and cocoa
an evening walk in the garden
a bedtime story with a concealed moral

the flaming sword
could have been a lantern held high
like that of an anxious mother
peering this way and that into the dark
calling too-late children home from play

her voice must have disappeared
into the dense blackness of evening
for children who would never return

whose story would be told
only in flyers tacked to utility poles
photos on milk cartons
and the big book of cautionary tales

wine on wings

happened one day last week

I was hurting
and the liquor store was closed

well there alone in my room
I heard a creak and looked up
to see an angel
easing in through the skylight
scraping off a couple of feathers
that drifted down on the air currents
in a shaft of sunlight

didn't stay

in and out

I hardly grasped what was
going on before it was over

getting out seemed a lot easier
I guess because the feathers
grew in the right direction for that

it just shot out slick as a whistle
leaving a gallon jug of cabernet
behind on the table

red wine

not a line of coke
and a rolled-up dollar bill
not a bottle of oxycodone
not a bag of herb
and some rolling papers
not a couple of cartons of rocky road
and a dozen krispy kremes
no it was a big jug of red
eight-ninety-nine a bottle
just what I always get

and then I remembered that no sparrow falls unseen

and there's an angel guarding every blade of grass

drenched and dripping world

"God is present
in every situation and every place."
        Metropolitan Anthony Bloom

yes I believe
that god is fully present
in the bread and wine

the problem is
I believe god is also fully present
in domino's pizza

the world
is so full of god
it's like melted butter
dripping onto your pancakes

the world is made of god
soaked with god
god clinging to your fingertips
you can't touch anything
without coming away with god hairs
all over you
like when you spend a lot of time
petting your dear old cat

who however beloved
leaves a trail of fur
all over the house
so that you can't even drink
a cup of coffee
without getting cat hair in your mouth

an analogy
the world is to god
as I am to macy's perfume samples
I leave smelling so redolent
of all that expensive free scent
that one cancels another out
I just have
a delicious aroma
called something like scent-o-rama
but the general effect is splendid
and you can smell me coming

god is:

like the malaysian buffet dinner
at merlin's hotel in hong kong
where you can just eat and eat and eat
until you think you'll never eat again
every variety of exotic seafood
that swims through water

like you're a big old hungry shark
that in addition scarfs down
fried rice and yorkshire pudding
like there's no tomorrow
then you walk back to your room
through the halls
with crooked damask wallpaper
drink gin
from the little fridge in your room
and sleep blissfully all afternoon

like the mountain of christmas presents
at your grandmother's house
the year you were eight
and she wrapped up every little thing
each one of the shoelaces
for your new pair of sneakers
was in its own fancy package
spangled with stars and silver ribbon

like one of those rainstorms
where the sky opens
and the rain smashes down
all in one second
as sharp and heavy as a guillotine
thunder making your blood stop
purple lightning crashing
into the ground all around

where you're standing
then a few minutes later
there's a gorgeous big rainbow
the sky is a tender blue
because you enjoyed it so much
a minute later it starts all over again

like when you were twenty
and you made love all night
and every time you came
and thought oh that was so good
I'll never need to do it again
ten minutes later you were at it
until you went to IHOP
for breakfast the next morning
and kept looking at each other
and laughing through the pecan waffles
and the waitress
and all the other people in the restaurant
were laughing with you
without any idea
of what was making you so happy

that's how I think of god
so I have no problem
believing
yes
god is fully present
in the bread and wine

do these examples
make it just a little bit clearer

after the duruflé requiem for all souls day

listen
we're just ordinary people
yet last night we invoked archangels
at st. mary's episcopal church
104 louella ave.
wayne pennsylvania
it's at an intersection
across from a construction site
something amazing happened there

we ate and drank god

the people in the church
well they're just people
sometimes angry or jealous or unfair
but nobody said hey you're not
good enough to be on friendly terms with god
it was like a potluck dinner
even if you aren't sure about somebody
you're willing to let them try your casserole
just to show your heart's in the right place
so everybody participated
anyway

we ate and drank god

ceremoniously using the best silver and crystal
flowers on the table candles
everybody dressed up
music reminding us
it wasn't going to go on forever
a time of rest and peace would come
no torment would ever touch us then
as a reminder

we ate and drank god

one helping seemed to satisfy everybody
at least I didn't see anybody lining up for seconds
saying I don't think the first time took
although I expect it would have been okay
that night in wayne when

we ate and drank god

I wondered about the priest
with total access to the host
would he be like a doctor
dipping into the narcotics cabinet
after a fight with his wife
or just a bad episode of depression
would he slip out
for an extra helping of wine and wafers
like standing before an open fridge at midnight

the light illuminating you
in the shadowed kitchen
eating that leftover chop
gulping a beer
then being able to get back into bed and sleep
the way we did that night

we ate and drank god

maybe wore god home
in those clouds of incense
clinging to our clothes as we danced lightly
through the streets
buoyant with blessing
infused with clouds of goodness
mingled then with other evening scents
the smoky blessing smell of burning leaves
the bakery redolent
of cinnamon and pesto parmesan
a neighbor smoking
on his shadowed porch
keeping his children's home smoke-free
his treat an inconsistent marijuana cigarette
from secret plants
he thinks no one has seen
among his flourishing tomato vines
a brief whiff of that pungency
enriched the mix

of god's incense and burning leaves and baking bread

that night we ate and drank god

scented so
when we got home wives and husbands
said there's something special in the air tonight
wrapped their arms around us in tight loving hugs
kissed us said let's get in bed and love
because you smell so good

not only that we said I'm full of god
you should have come
I'll bet it was more exciting than your adventure movie

listen we ate and drank god

Nina Corwin

Outpatient Suite

I seem to myself, as in a dream,
An accidental guest in this dreadful body.
— Anna Akhmatova

It is in moments of illness that we are compelled to recognize that we live not alone but chained to a creature of a different kingdom, whole worlds apart, who has no knowledge of us and by whom it is impossible to make ourselves understood: our body.
— Marcel Proust

*Oh Doctor, please help me, I'm damaged.
There's a pain where there once was a heart...*
– Mick Jagger/Keith Richards

i. To Begin With

For a month at least.   I haven't been myself.
>A touch of flu, a bit of rash, a rush
>>of rivers in my ears.

Today I noticed a sort of swelling
>like foreign bodies in my body.

It's hard to explain, doctor,
>but I hoped you could
>>give it a look.

ii. Muffle

    This may sound strange, doctor, but
lately the idle of trucks at the stop
        light rumbles like nobody's business.
    Song birds muffled or mum.

But at night
        it gets so hushed   I can hear
the sound of telephones before they ring.
        Rattle of stars.   Far away hoofs.

    Last week, I thought I heard a huddle
        of rats planning their next offensive.

What does it mean, doc?
        Can you make it go away?

iii. Manners

How rude of me not to ask.　How *is* the family?
    I love your tie, by the way: the syringes,
        the stethoscopes. Very smart.

iv. On Further Inquiry

Sometimes I wake up feeling like a wind-up toy,
> heart-shaped key in my back.

> > Stiffness: Yes.
> > Spinning: You mean me or the room?
> > Ringing in my ears: Not exactly –

More like invisible cymbals
> erupting in clang associations.
Primitive winds drumming
> up from the south.

v. *It's All In the Chart*

Listen doctor   I've endured

a string of unfortunate touches
some pinches   some needles   and now

I've been crosshaired and groped
                    at your behest:

    Shook up in the morning

    Shook down before bed
                        and thensome.

The staff confirms it: Touched, they say.

vi. Tripping

More and more I get this feeling I'm about to
    take a fall.
Like my feet are sinking into fog. I fall
    for everything, doctor. Everything
        's turning to quicksand. Or cotton.

Like   gravity's got a thing for me.
        Like   somebody stole the high notes.

vii. Parts

Did you hear the one about the surgeon
                      left a music box behind
        when he stitched his patient up?

                Maybe somebody left
some pieces out when they put me back together?

                        Like a watch or a toaster.

                      [you asked for blood and I gave it —
                            I've done my part]

viii. Immunity

Doctor Untouched and Doctor Unflappable.
Doctor Well-dressed and Well-rehearsed.
> Are you always so immune?

You say oops like I can't hear you.
> Oops below   (with knife and fork).

> > There, there   you say.
> > > There. Right. There.

Doctor Masked and Doctor Scrubbed.
Doctor Gloved and High-handed:
> Do you inhale while you work?

   Are your probes really probative? Doctor
Your Nose in Decision Trees   GOD
DAMN IT   TALK TO ME

ix.

[silence]

x. What Am I Paying You For?

Here we go again with your signs and symptoms.
Here we go again with your lists of criteria.

> Playing Spin-the-platelets
> Playing Dial-a-diagnosis.

You tell me what it isn't. Rule out the customary perils.

> Shall I feel better now?

x+1. Parasite

Let's play Daisy-Do: He cures me, he cures me not.
    Name that parasite. Pin the fix on the fixer.

    Let me give you a hand. See
                if you can count the lines.

riddle me this, doc:
if a tree rots in the forest and the bloodwork doesn't tell
is the patient invisible?

xii. Really?

    I'm not making this up.

There were times I lied, it's true. I didn't want to
go to gym. The teacher was mean. I mean
drill sergeant mean.
    She called us Chicken Fat   sweated us
up
in those stupid bloomers.   As for my stomach
        it DID kind of hurt.
           But That isn't This.

I have to admit, though, the worse things get
I wonder is it me makes it so.
Like I touch myself while I sleep and wake up
with welts.

xiii. Epistemology

Please tell your pal, Doctor Occam: Sometimes
those hoof-beats are zebras, not horses.
Sometimes the razor cuts both ways.

xiv. There Must Be a Pill For This

      Something from your closet
beneath the stairs.   Something not so toxic.
          A sample. A trial. A lark.
                  Pretty please?

I've seen bottles with happy-faces on the label.
        Bottles with bull's-eyes.

Or better: a dose
of your best bedside manner. Give me
      a smile perhaps, a little
      laying on of hands

xv. Too Much Information

I've been poking around the internet. Trying to figure it out.

Looking up actions and re-actions.

Click

Looking up outcomes.

Click

They advise in the sidebars with bullets.

Advise with standard deviations.

Acres of fine print.   *<scroll down>*

Warnings in boldface.

Double click

It's scary but I can't stop looking.

xvi. In Medias REM

Last night I dreamt the realest dream:
Caged monkeys were in it. Gears without teeth
        and you, of course.
    Pointing cartoon arrows every which.

Me and Beethoven are playing
        duets in a labyrinth.
Then the scene peels.   The road narrows.
    I stutter into second, fluids leaking,
        chassis misaligned.

    The point is, I'm trying to find a mechanic
but I can't even make the end of the block.
    The point is, doctor, what I need is a tow.

xoxo. *Hey*

Doc, has anyone told you you look like Jekyll?

Am I Heckle, doc?

Am I hide or hair?

Am I losing it all?

xviii. What Next?

Yesterday I saw a man without feet selling pencils.
A girl in epileptic's helmet, chapped hands a-tremor.

I couldn't help it –
I had to cross the street: I kept thinking in triptychs.

Three's a charm you know:

    Contagion. Stop watch. Gangplank.

[What's that you're writing?]

xix. LISTEN

Doc, I've got tears breaking into pieces here.
I've got birds in my sternum creating a flap

Comets slamming into other comets;
                failed stars singing failed arias

I can feel the trees falling around me.
                Are they making sounds?

xx. *Please, Doctor, Don't*

send me home with holes in my hands

>> You've got to DO something
> (twist a dial, stop   the river
>> leaking through   the rising silence)

I can't hear you doctor. I can't hear.

I can't

Jason Gordon

Attack of the Nihilist

Holding Myself for Ransom

I have no lungs

I breathe by
opening and
closing my fists

*

I can throw a pumpkin full of explosives
into the kitchen.

I can crush a cube of frozen paint thinner in my
  hand,
lay down on a domino the size of a mattress.

I can rip apart the garden shears
like a wishbone—

angels bouncing between spark plugs,
smoke doing its rain dance around the room:

no one will notice.
The sun is a junkie's eyeball and

rats stampede through the neighborhood.
I play chess against myself.

Every black pawn I take
I have to swallow.

*

It takes years to write one report days to write one
   word seconds to write one life story.

I make up all my memories—
a blizzard of stars swallowing every weatherman
not armed with an umbrella. Which beers

taste less bad? How do I pry
the inner-squirrel from my finger and
who sent this arresting bouquet
of snorkels? Death?

The grandfather clock
sinks deep into the floor,
its white roots gripping the pipes
like an octopus. I break

and un-break the dishes.

*

It's the same every morning:
the house folds itself up like a map when I leave it,
static infecting the radio.

I wake the avocado not a real avocado
one from the garden where our ghosts hide.

I'm bored with my eyes,
I close them open them pull off my lips kiss my
   own nose,
the salad tongs in my hand.

Neuropoem

1.
The living zombie in the machine I call home wears
   my pants.
Not me I've been never that stoned. I have even
   ideas.
I die I go to China where I learn to make chickens.
I get seasick reading poems about boats, wake up
naked next to a woman I assume is my wife. She's
not the Great Wall. She vomits pink foam, I eat my
   own brain.

2.
I unfold my brain and crumple it into a ball.
My brain is a paper swan that wants to be a real swan.
A ganglia of morons. It eats this poem
it vomits this poem. This poem isn't edible.
It can't lie or tell the truth. Ask me about this poem,
this peom. Pretend your brain loves mine
or my brain hates cures. Yours thinks
better than mine, types fast with slow errors.
It's not also worse at perpendicular parking.

Attack of the Nihilist

1.
No one can see the future,
not even people
with owls on their heads; but

I can make lightning
strike the barn.

I can fill a boot
with sawdust and
grab a fistful of
white beetles
from my pocket.

What can you do?

2.
The only cloud—
a big cat. It yawns until
its jaws bend backwards and
it swallows its own head.
We often exchange
yawns on the phone.
The star of sex
fades in your eyes;

the dream lays its black
eggs in your hair.
Dust settles on the furniture
of my life. I look out the window:
a swarm of bees
in the shape of a man
walks a puppy down the sidewalk.

3.
You wake up at midnight; the moths
fluttering around the moon,
the moths of your dream, already
begin to fade. There is nothing you can do.
You close your eyes; there is only
darkness, so cold not even
candles of bone could survive.

You stare at the ceiling
which stares back like
the blank page of a book.

4.
The stars carve circles in the sky
like grooves in a record.
Music makes the clouds sad;
they sink into the earth
like the ghosts of our furniture.

But one of them sneaks into
my room while I sleep,
fogging up the mirror with
its breath, placing stones soaked
in moon blood all around my bed.

In the morning I find blue footprints on the ceiling.

5.
A field with grass so dead
a downpour of angel tears
couldn't revive it. That's where
dreams go when we forget them—

tornados searching for
empty wine bottles to sleep in.

The clouds eat the stars.

6.
The mind is a dark ocean of voices.

I hear screams; the pinecones
explode like grenades.
The flying squirrels slowly
glide to earth, then
they explode too.

The chandelier swings wildly in my heart.
I stick a fork in my thigh
and somewhere in India
my pain appears on a map.

So many emaciated cows;
the milkman rings the doorbell but
there is no door, not even
a window to climb through.

The moon drops grand pianos from its eyes.

Cave Drawings

man eats animal
man eats spirit animal

---

so many dimensions in the universe

only one dream passing from room
to room peeling paint off walls
exposing cave drawings from the future

or infinite dreams
filling one room
with smoke

I close my eyes I no longer exist
I exist in the dimension of god dog particles

---

the lady in the moon grows a long
beard of chains there are non-existent
clouds a light bulb crushed into

snow on the lawn I am trying not
to breathe or use the phone to
burn the mind it cannot have
ideas birds flapping in my soup

---

the phone is dead
the phone isn't dead

the gods are wireless

---

my hands build a bird
out of rare flying books

I can't find my gloves
my nails are mirrors

I piss in the sink

Cheat Codes

It's still December still July
a blue cloud walks a dog across the lake

my hands fall off
I glue them back on
my head falls off
I warm it in the oven

I no longer exist I will
exist again tomorrow
I can't remember
my name can you
remember my name?

it's cold in the microwave

*

the pillow swallows my head

but my mind with its tentacles
rests on a nest
of crumpling un-crumpling poems

or it sits on the tv and stares at
the tree growing out of the sofa

it doesn't wear pants it can't
think or hum songs from the 80s

too much not enough
synthesized drums

too asleep too awake

it can't decide

*

Even dogs have feelings even fleas
but fleas are not important
the Stanley Cup is important
energy drinks are important
lighter fluid is important it makes
fire for smoking pot and pot is
important God is important
he has feelings he has blue
fleas in his beard this isn't
the 60s or it is he can't tell
time his bones dance on the sea

*

You steal my hubcaps
I buy them back
you eat a peach

with a fork made of blood
it's an old heart it weeps
each tear is a seed
or a metaphor for something maybe
love or the sadness of trees
leaves shaped like hands
hands shaped like leaves

your hubcaps my hubcaps

inner-child outer-child
mirror image
reflection
it's a roadmap crumpling
un-crumpling in the dark

*

I won't look in the mirror my reflection
is a vampire with acne and prescription sunglasses
he stays up all day dreaming writing
poems about nothing he's not
my mirror image he will never
taste lobster dipped in blood or bend
his fork into a bracelet for you to
re-gift like his heart covered in flies

*

I try not to explode
or microwave the dog

but sometimes the universe
is fucked-up static
a blizzard of stars
antimatter moonlight

so dead it's alive
and infested with clouds

angry clouds full of lightning and snow

cold dandruff
yellow cocaine

angels vacuuming
the lawn I try not
to snort them I try

*

the sky is dead

no seeds in the glass
cubes of its teeth

an endless landscape of hiccups

the occasional iceberg
of sunlight taps on the window

oh blank dance of clouds
the porch is on fire
the milk strings of your guitar

shatter on the roof

Weathervanes

The lady in the moon
looks pissed. The clouds
of her breath chase
cars into the lake.

The salmon swim backwards

*

The future is broken
Fighter jets disguised as geese assume their
   checkmark formation
The clouds sink like battleships into the grass
O say can you pee, laughs my inner-child, peeing
Not so funny to the outer-child, prostate swollen,
   back hair gathering frost

A rose of butter hardens
The beehives die, the snails ask questions

*

My eye isn't naked,
it wears tiny shoes.

It dances all night
in a puddle of merlot.

Not drunk, not a stone
with quartz teeth

biting the dentist.
This isn't a love poem.

The TV is off, the screen
is a mirror. The dead

leap from clouds shaped like airliners—
falling bodies of rain

*

I hate rain. I sink through
hours of darkness, passing only
the occasional neon jellyfish.
My bed lands on the moon,
the moon lands on my bed.
It doesn't matter. A cloud
coughs down the door.
I weep, pull a dark quilt
of porn over my eyes.
The dog eats me. Showers
melt the town I grew up in:
the idiot weatherman, his umbrella
opening, closing itself at will

Oneirology

1.
The window is open, just enough
to let the wind come in,
toss some old receipts on the floor,
chase the cat from the bedroom,
turn on the TV. The rest of the house

is asleep, a dream passing from room
to room like a swarm of ghost bees.
It's a sad dream, one that's survived
hundreds of years, feeding on dead mice
and the occasional lost tennis shoe.

Every wall is a different shade of static.

2.
Sleep provides energy for the day's undertakings
such as shopping for a new spice rack
or chiseling cat mucus off the kitchen floor with a butter knife,
but come nightfall that energy funnels down the cosmic drain
into a dimension where we are all statues
and our voices are red birds that fly from our mouths.
I sit alone in my cave trying to write poetry but

all that comes from my brain is
nonsense: a white bib forgetting
its own tragic lullaby, some shiny butter snails,
a villa sketched by madmen
pounded into a small cube, then one night
a bright slit appears in the sky
and out spew the stars
followed by pink clouds of dust
inside which angels are born like
corn popping in the microwave.

3.
It's stupid to believe in miracles.
If threatened, an angel will fall from the sky,
not a sky you want on a picnic
this sky will bite off your leg!
So can there be joy?
The cervix melts like butter,
the baby oozes out.

4.
I love the beach even though it's a giant litter box/
    ashtray.
Ocean noise sounds like radio static, the womb
minus the bass drum of mother's heartbeat.
Sometimes the sand burns my feet but
have you been to the beach when it's cold,
wind blowing out the birthday cakes
in your eyes? It's not Dorothy's Kansas

or the bingo hall of the underworld it's
a postcard written by statues, something wrong
with the clouds so the weatherman unscrambles
   eggs on his desk.

5.
Is this how the world ends, angels inside us
multiplying like viruses, microwaving our bones?

We burn our inner-children, feed our laundry to the
   moon,
die asleep on memory foam. No one remembers.

You press the up button, the elevator never arrives.
Is the lobby all that exists

or is there a malfunction in the heavens,
a hand-shaped weed poking up through the sidewalk?

Pain rises from deep inside the earth.
Mirrors shatter, reading glasses on the floor

like stepped-on grasshoppers. So what's
an old book to do? Swallow a hurricane?

If one writes a book on this side of the mirror
on the other side there must exist the opposite of
   that book—

a book you can read in the dark, a book
made of snow. The roller coasters untangle
  themselves.

6.
The angel in the phone line swims backwards. I've
un-dreamt my life: half dead, half drunk. One
morning I'm a cloud in my father's belly; the next a
ghost, a spray of cologne. The scent of the moon
making love to the sea. The scent of two storms
making love on the beach. I can't decide. The
angel swims forwards, backwards at the speed of
darkness. The more I drink, the louder the dial
tone.

7.
I'm born I'm unborn
I'm born again
I'm dead I'm undead
I splash coffee on my face, drink a bottle of
  mouthwash for breakfast
I ejaculate my sorrows into the sink
Into the sea
Sperm the size of whales, whales the size of sperm
I love I hate I love myself
I love my father I hate my father
I am my father

Whales in my belly
God in my beard

8.
I can't sleep; I'm becoming
an owl, an owl with moon-eyes,
an owl who eats pizza for breakfast,
cold pizza with mushrooms of blood.

I disassemble the cuckoo clock
in its nest of brass twigs.

Us Men in Suits

for Travis

The lit elevator button
turned into a glowing moth.
We ducked and shielded
our faces until it landed
on a little girl's finger.
"There's nothing to be afraid of,"
she said, before it
coughed out a tiny
puff of black smoke.

Oh how we screamed.

Biographies & Acknowledgments

Tree Riesener is the author of *Sleepers Awake*, a collection of fiction, winner of the Eludia Award, Sowilo Press; *The Hubble Cantos*, Aldrich Press; and *EK*, to be published in early 2017 by Cervena Barva Press; three previous chapbooks: *Liminalog,* a collection of ghazals and sijo, *Inscapes*, and A*ngel Poison*. Former Managing Editor of the Schuylkill Valley Journal and former Contributing Editor to The Ghazal Page, she is on Facebook and Twitter, and loves to hear from readers. Her website is www.treeriesener.com.

Nina Corwin is the author of *The Uncertainty of Maps* (CW Books) and *Conversations With Friendly Demons and Tainted Saints* (Puddin'head Press), as well as two chap-books: *Dear Future* (Glass Lyre Press) and *What to Pack for the Apocalypse* (Locofo Chaps). Her poetry has appeared in *Drunken Boat, Harvard Review, Hotel Amerika, New Ohio Review/nor, Sou-thern Poetry Review and Verse*. She curates the literary series at Chicago's Woman Made Gallery and in daytime hours, she is a psychotherapist known for her work on behalf of victims of violence.

Jason Gordon earned an MFA from the University of Maryland, as well as a scholarship to the Bread Loaf Writers' Conference. One of the included poems is from his chapbook, *I Stole a Briefcase* (Pudding House Press). He lives in Catonsville, Maryland, teaching English and creative writing at a middle school for children with dyslexia. Some of the included poems previously appeared in *yes, Poetry, Cutbank, Presa, Pretty Owl* and *Skidrow Penthouse*.